”

For You

The German National Library lists this publication in the German National Bibliography;
detailed bibliographic data is available on the Internet at www.dnb.de.

365 Quotes for a Daily Dose of Dry Humor: Satirical and Sarcastic Sayings for Every Day
(Your Daily Dose of Sarcasm and Irony on the Madness of our World Today) by Tim Reichel

Impact Verlag, Studienscheiss GmbH
Oppenhoffallee 143, 52066 Aachen
kontakt@studienscheiss.de
Managing Director: Dr. Tim Reichel, M. Sc.
Registry court: Local Court Aachen
Registration number: HRB 19105
VAT ID No.: DE295455486

1st edition, December 2023

ISBN: 978-3-98597-152-7 Print (Softcover)
ISBN: 978-3-98597-153-4 E-Book (PDF)
ISBN: 978-3-98597-154-1 E-Book (EPUB)

Copy editing and proofreading: Delia Hansen, Piet Retief
Editor: Hannah Dautzenberg, Aachen
Cover design: Melanie Schwarz, Aachen
Cover illustration: ucla_pucla / shutterstock.com
Photo: Sajoscha Blinn, Bottrop
Manufacturer: Amazon
Printed in Germany

”

365 Quotes

for

A Daily Dose of Dry Humor

Tim Reichel

Impact Verlag

Preface

Always have a suitable quip in stock

Whether in everyday life or on special occasions: An apt quote can save any situation and provide new momentum in life. However, if you want to stand out from the crowd and show character, you need to be original. Stale proverbs like "Give every day the chance to be the best day of your life" won't lure even the most loyal of dogs out from his kennel. This is because these well-meant sayings have become boring and predictable – the proverbial cliché. Some even go so far as to describe them as mendacious empty phrases that have lost all meaning in the age of wall tattoos and Facebook slogans.

That's why I suggest a different approach: humor. Brutally truthful and slightly mean humor, to be precise. Instead of tormenting your fellow human beings with corny positive banter, you can provoke them to deeper thoughts by handing out these little severities. An atrocious quip at the right time invigorates every relationship, shakes things up and creates a new perspective. It's not about offending the other person (at least not permanently), but solely about the surprising impetus and the unexpected shared joy of a little bluntness.

That's why I've written this book for you and researched, translated and prepared 365 merciless quotes for you which you can use to dispense little pieces of wisdom every day. Use them to bring a breath of fresh air into your own life or to share your loving mischievousness with others. These quotes come from writers, politicians, scientists, actors, artists and other important personalities. In short: from successful people who have achieved great things and developed a passion for sarcastic remarks and subtle satirical jibes. I would like to pass this curious collection on to you so that you can pick up a new daily dose of alternative humor and use it to fight back against the madness of this world every day.

Although I have assigned each quote to a specific date, this does not mean that you have to follow my preselection. You can read the book in a criss-cross fashion and remind yourself of your favorite sayings again and again. I have also clustered the quotes according to themes so that you can quickly find the most suitable words for special occasions such as birthdays, weddings or family celebrations.

In addition to the 365 quotes, I have a little surprise for you. I've put together a total of 100 more quotes that unfortunately didn't make it into this book due to lack of space. On the last page you will find a link to this collection. It will take you to my website where you can register for the gift – free of charge, of course.

Almost every day we deal with people who could do with a little food for thought. We should help them – and the best way to do this is with a little satire. The next time you want to "surprise" your partner, your colleague at the office is annoying or you need a little cheering up yourself, you can open this treasure, read a few lines and then get going with renewed energy. Have fun with it!

Tim Reichel

January

January 1st

Year: A period of
three hundred and sixty-five disappointments.

Ambrose Bierce

January 2nd

The path to the goal is never straight,
but it's not crooked either.
In fact, it doesn't exist at all.

Susan Sontag

January 3rd

If you're slow, you'll get there too,
just later than everyone else.

Jesse Owens

January 4th

Other people also want to have a hard time.
We should help them with that.

Paul Watzlawick

January 5th

If you want to help the poor,
demonstrate to them that they can become rich;
prove it by getting rich yourself.

🗩 *Wallace Wattles*

January 6th

I do not believe in progress,
but in the persistence of human stupidity.

🗩 *Oscar Wilde*

January 7th

Two things are infinite:
the universe and human stupidity;
and I'm not sure about the universe.

🗩 *Albert Einstein*

January 8th

Love is being stupid together.

🗩 *Paul Valéry*

January 9th

Nothings is more gratifying than finding the person
you can tease for the rest of your life.

Agatha Christie

January 10th

Love isn't there to make us happy.
I believe it exists to show us
how much we can endure.

Hermann Hesse

January 11th

Anyone who believes
that marriage makes you happy
simply hasn't found the right partner yet.

Jane Austen

January 12th

The most valuable thing in life is the time
when our partner is absent.

Vivien Leigh

January 13th

My wife doesn't care what I do when I'm away,
as long as I don't have a good time.

Lee Trevino

January 14th

A hundred litte pinpricks
are a thousand times more fun
than one big one.

Shirley MacLaine

January 15th

An intelligent man sometimes needs to
be drunk to spend time with idiots.

Ernest Hemingway

January 16th

Friends are God's way of
apologizing to us for our families.

Tennessee Williams

January 17th

Whoever thinks that Jesus came to the people voluntarily,
doesn't know his father well.

Gilbert Keith Chesterton

January 18th

The first half of our lives are ruined by our parents
and the second half by our children.

Clarence Darrow

January 19th

In a marriage, children are like
flies in your soup.

Robert Crumb

January 20th

Every time I meet my inner child,
it gets a resounding slap in the face.

Anthony Burgess

January 21st

Only those who retain a childlike sense of wonder
are easy to deceive.

Margaret Thatcher

January 22nd

When you fool a fool
you strike a blow for intelligence.

Giacomo Casanova

January 23rd

Women, as a rule, choose a nightgown for themselves
much more carefully than their husband.

Coco Chanel

January 24th

The secret of a good marriage
is forgiving your partner for marrying you
in the first place.

Sacha Guitry

January 25th

I've had bad luck in my two previous marriages.
The first wife left me, and the second did not.

Woody Allen

January 26th

Most husbands are proof
that women have a sense of humor.

Donna Leon

January 27th

Never doubt your wife's good judgement.
After all, she married a genius.

Federico Fellini

January 28th

Only the male intellect,
clouded by sexual drive, could call the wide-hipped
and short-legged sex beautiful.

Arthur Schopenhauer

January 29th

The average women would rather
have beauty than brains, because the average man
can see better than he can think.

💬 *Mark Twain*

January 30th

A gentleman is one
who never swears at his wife
when ladies are present.

💬 *Alec Guinness*

January 31st

If there is anyone here
whom I have not insulted,
I beg your pardon.

💬 *Johannes Brahms*

February

February 1st

A day that starts in the morning
can never be good.

Ernest Hemingway

February 2nd

If a woman is punctual to the minute,
she has the wrong day.

Georg Thomalla

February 3rd

Behind the life of each individual
there is a divine error.

Rajav Singh

February 4th

Life is short and we never find enough time
to harass our companions.

Walter Serner

February 5th

Annoying yourself is fun.
Annoying others makes you happy.

💬 *Li Bai*

February 6th

Luck is when bad luck hits others.

💬 *Horaz*

February 7th

Nothing gives as much pleasure
as awakening the loser in others.

💬 *Garri Kimowitsch Kasparow*

February 8th

Sometimes, you lose
and sometimes the others win.

💬 *Otto Rehhagel*

February 9th

Winning is nice, but the real pleasure
lies in consoling the losers.

Desmond Tutu

February 10th

Children are not only a consolation for old age,
but also a means of reaching it more quickly.

Roberto Benigni

February 11th

In old age, children are a comfort
as long as they don't come to visit you.

Sarah Bernhardt

February 12th

Of all the guests, the ones
I like best are those who break down
on the trip and cancel.

Thomas Mann

February 13th

Some people bring joy wherever they go,
and some people bring joy whenever they go.

Mark Twain

February 14th

If the time is right,
the place is usually wrong.

Agnetha Fältskog

February 15th

You do women an injustice if you say
they always finish too late, it's not true.
They only start too late.

Moritz Gottlieb Saphir

February 16th

Perseverance is rewarded
sooner or later – but usually later.

Wilhelm Busch

February 17th

You have to think for a while to realize
that you are unhappy, but it's worth it.

Shirley Bassey

February 18th

Only people who think positively
stand out truly negatively.

Stephen King

February 19th

Nothing in the world is as wonderfully
contagious as a bad mood.

Charles Dickens

February 20th

A contagious disease is the
only thing you can pass on without losing it.

Robert Gallo

February 21st

What good is health,
if you're an idiot?

Theodor Adorno

February 22nd

If you want to grow old, you have to
disinherit your descendants.

Elizabeth George

February 23rd

Only a fool celebrates getting older.

George Bernard Shaw

February 24th

Gladly I remember the times,
when all limbs where limber – except for one.
But the times are over,
all limbs have become stiff – except for one.

Johann Wolfgang von Goethe

February 25th

Whoever retains the ability
to dish out malice will never grow old.

Konrad Adenauer

February 26th

Malice is to the mind
what gymnastics is to the body.

Ludwig Börne

February 27th

Even the stupid sometimes has a clever thought.
They just don't realize it.

Danny Kaye

February 28th

Often you see something
a hundred times before you realize
how uninteresting it is.

Henri Matisse

February 29th

Never try to make someone
as you are yourself.
You should know that
one of your kind is enough.

Ralph Waldo Emerson

”

March

March 1st

Forgiving the other for being different
is the beginning of all evil.

Honoré de Mirabeau

March 2nd

Those who forgive their neighbors
are just too lazy to argue.

Johannes Gross

March 3rd

Not to be born is
undoubtedly the best plan of all.

Emile Cioran

March 4th

You have to ask yourself about
some conversation participants: do they actually help
with the solution or do they belong to the problem?

Robert Jungk

March 5th

People who reach the top of the tree
are only those who haven't got the qualifications
to be detained them at the bottom.

Peter Ustinov

March 6th

You can recognize the really great
people by the fact that they do nothing.

Roswitha von Gandersheim

March 7th

The secret of
success is to get up early,
work late and strike oil.

John Davison Rockefeller

March 8th

Everything is easy before it is difficult.

Erich Honecker

March 9th

An easy life has never been good for anyone.

Hildegard von Bingen

March 10th

Those who don't have a beautiful life
can still hope for a beautiful death.

Ian Fleming

March 11th

Most people become likeable
only after they die.

Martin Heidegger

March 12th

Flowers bring the most joy
when you can put them on someone's coffin.

Stephen King

March 13th

If you want to be scolded, get married;
if you want to be praised, die.

💬 *Flann O'Brien*

March 14th

Some men who you think have been dead
for a long time are merely married.

💬 *Peter Sellers*

March 15th

The greates military achievement
of the century is my marriage.

💬 *Friedrich Dürrenmatt*

March 16th

Any married man should
forget his mistakes – there's no use in two people
remembering the same thing.

💬 *John Calvin Maxwell*

March 17th

Remind your fellow men
of their worries and your heart will be light.

Jeremias Gotthelf

March 18th

You never know what's going to happen in this world.
I'll just keep my mouth shut. That's a good idea.

Masahiro Sakurai

March 19th

Wise people are often silent.
And when they do say something,
their fatally bad breath is always noticeable.

Frank Zappa

March 20th

If you don't know anything bad to say about someone else,
better not say anything at all.

Jane Austen

March 21st

If there were no bad people,
there would be no good lawyers.

Charles Dickens

March 22nd

The greatest advantage is gained
by those who trip others up.

Benjamin Disraeli

March 23rd

The most wasteful day of all
is the day you couldn't laugh
at someone else's misfortune.

Nicolas Chamfort

March 24th

Evil people can be counted on.
At least they don't change.

William Faulkner

March 25th

Whoever believes that he will develop
will become even worse than he already was.

Philip Roth

March 26th

The only thing that you can change in the world
is the position of your pillow.

Gabriel García Márquez

March 27th

Hopefully you never wanted to become
the way you have.

Carl Gustav Jung

March 28th

Beautiful weather always
belies the real situation.

Paul Gauguin

March 29th

Nothing is more
disappointing than some people
getting off lightly.

Agatha Christie

March 30th

When other people are happy
we should point out to them that everything
positive has a downside.

Francoise Sagan

March 31st

Happy people are not happy,
they are stupid.

Voltaire

April

April 1st

In our time there is a lot of talk
about irony and humor, especially by people
who have never been able to practice it.

Søren Kierkegaard

April 2nd

The only correct attitude to today's world
is that of cultivated black humor.

Georg Kreisler

April 3rd

All the harm in the world comes from people
who think they have to do something good.

Arthur Koestler

April 4th

Good people die young, bad people live a little longer.

Charles Laughton

April 5th

Most people would rather die
than think: many do.

Bertrand Russell

April 6th

Many would never speak
with a full mouth, but do it
with an empty head.

Orson Welles

April 7th

It's easier to nod with an empty head.

Žarko Petan

April 8th

Better to remain silent
and be thought a fool than to speak out
and remove all doubt.

Abraham Lincoln

April 9th

We appreciate people
who speak their minds freshly and openly –
provided they say the same thing we do.

Mark Twain

April 10th

The truth is like a wet towel.
It's no use to you, but you can wrap it
around someone else's head.

Elizabeth George

April 11th

There are two ways to make a career.
Either you really achieve something
or you claim to achieve something.
I recommend the first method, because there
is not nearly as much competition.

Danny Kaye

April 12th

In every organization,
there is a person who knows.
That person must be discovered and fired,
otherwise the organization cannot function.

💬 *Cyril Northcote Parkinson*

April 13th

Those who have talent rarely
have the decency to spare others with it.

💬 *Elvis Costello*

April 14th

Stupidity is also a natural talent.

💬 *Wilhelm Busch*

April 15th

One's own stupidity is only fun
when others also shine their light on it.

💬 *Jacques Tati*

April 16th

The happiness of others can make
the most cheerful man gloomy.

Truman Capote

April 17th

Whenever you think you can't carry on anymore,
a misfortune happens to someone else
and you are happy again.

Daphne du Maurier

April 18th

Those who have no goal in life itself
can at least destroy the progress of others.

Benjamin Franklin

April 19th

More enjoyable than being ambitious is
seeing an ambitious person fail.

Boris Vian

April 20th

Watching former partners
fail is a wonderful pleasure.

Zsa Zsa Gabor

April 21st

The secret of a happy marriage
remains a secret.

Henny Youngman

April 22nd

The longer one is married,
the more incomprehensible it becomes
how one could have been so deceived.

Phyllis Dorothy James

April 23rd

What does it mean when you come home to a man
who gives you love, affection and tenderness?
It means that you are at the wrong door.

Bette Midler

April 24th

If you are looking for a good,
understanding and beautiful woman,
you are looking for not one, but three.

Oscar Wilde

April 25th

Happiness is like a pair of glasses.
You look for it until you step on it
and then it's gone.

Annette von Droste-Hülshoff

April 26th

If you want something very badly,
you can be sure you'll never get it.

Roald Dahl

April 27th

Anyone who is satisfied is doing something wrong.

Bernhard von Clairvaux

April 28th

I will be satisfied if my next marriage
outlasts the shelf life of yogurt.

Elizabeth Taylor

April 29th

When a relationship is too much fun,
you should talk about it.

Yves Montand

April 30th

A woman abhors rude behaviour,
she gently castrates her husband by criticising him.

Catherine Millet

May

May 1st

If you pray in the morning,
you have the rest of the day for fun.

Marilyn Monroe

May 2nd

Abundant sinning is
the source of all pleasant memories.

Georges Bernanos

May 3rd

Those who act piously
are only too weak to sin.

Anna Magnani

May 4th

There may be better
air in heaven, but there is certainly
better company in hell.

George Bernard Shaw

May 5th

What they do in heaven we are ignorant of;
but what they do not do we are told expressly;
they neither marry nor are given in marriage.

🗩 *Jonathan Swift*

May 6th

They say marriages are made in heaven.
But so is thunder and lightning.

🗩 *Clint Eastwood*

May 7th

The best experts on women are the meterologists:
They give the hurricanes women's names.

🗩 *Peter Ustinov*

May 8th

To err may be masculine,
but to experience disaster requires a woman.

🗩 *Curd Jürgens*

May 9th

A good wife always forgives
her husband when she's wrong.

Milton Berle

May 10th

A wife supports us in crises
that we would not have gotten into
at all without her.

Danny DeVito

May 11th

A romantic weekend for two
can ruin the strongest man.

George Clooney

May 12th

Women like simple things
in life: men.

Farrah Fawcett

May 13th

Men are like a fine wine. They all start out like grapes,
and it's our job to stomp on them and keep them in the dark until they mature into something you'd like to have dinner with.

Jill Shalivs

May 14th

The majority of husbands remind me of
an orangutan trying to play the violin.

Honoré de Balzac

May 15th

In the animal kingdom, the males are more beautiful than the females.
God has corrected this error in human beings.

Claudia Bini

May 16th

Man was made at the end of
the week's work when God was tired.

Mark Twain

May 17th

Unpleasant tasks become more exciting
if you move them to the end of the day.

Ivan Illich

May 18th

Those who still talk while the others start work
relax and live longer.

Charles Bukowski

May 19th

Morality is when you live in such a way
that living that way isn't any fun.

Édith Piaf

May 20th

Learning something good is an effort;
learning something bad is fun.

Jacques Tati

May 21st

You can't teach anyone anything,
but you can get paid for it.

Ephraim Kishon

May 22nd

Strangers get to know the city better
if you give them the wrong directions.

Helmut Qualtinger

May 23rd

The road to success is paved
with other people's failures.

Doris Lessing

May 24th

The success of close friends is bitter,
especially when it could have been prevented.

Howard Hughes

May 25th

Success rises to the head only
if there is the necessary cavity.

Manfred Hinrich

May 26th

Success goes to people's heads,
but the worst effect is usually
on the abdominal area.

Orson Welles

May 27th

People who have a good heart
almost always have a bad figure.

Jean Harlow

May 28th

Only those who think negatively
from the heart can be positively suprised.

Albert Einstein

May 29th

Those who search for happiness within experiences a nasty surprise.

🗨 *Friedrich Nietzsche*

May 30th

Nobody is able to to lead you astray as reliably as your inner voice.

🗨 *Anaïs Nin*

May 31st

Take courage! Whatever you decide to do, it will probably be the wrong thing.

🗨 *Ashleigh Brilliant*

June

June 1st

The rising of the sun
is an imposition every time.

Honoré de Balzac

June 2nd

When something stupid is said,
it becomes light in the hearts of men.

Voltaire

June 3rd

Never laugh at the stupidity of others
– it is your chance.

Winston Churchill

June 4th

Never interrupt your enemy
when he is making a mistake.

Napoleon Bonaparte

June 5th

Forgive your enemies,
but never forget their names.

John Fitzgerald Kennedy

June 6th

We should forgive our enemies,
but not before they are hanged.

Heinrich Heine

June 7th

Nothing is nobler than forgiving
wrongdoings that do not concern us.

Franziska zu Reventlow

June 8th

Sincerty is the
form of stupidity.

Karl Liebknecht

June 9th

Power without abuse
loses its charm.

Paul Valéry

June 10th

Many women don't know what they want
but they are determined to get it.

Peter Ustinov

June 11th

You don't have to signal a
social conscience by looking like a frump.

Elizabeth Bibesco

June 12th

Sweatpants are a sign of defeat.
You lost control of your life so you
bought some sweatpants.

Karl Lagerfeld

June 13th

It is the encounters with people
that make life so dull.

Jack London

June 14th

I'm in love with cities I've never been to
and people I've never met.

Melody Truong

June 15th

I learned the most from people in my life
who had exactly the same opinion as I did.

Bertrand Russell

June 16th

I love people who freely say
what they think – as long as they think
the same as I do.

Muhammad Ali

June 17th

All people are allowed to think,
but many are spared it.

Curt Goetz

June 18th

Think what is true, feel what is beautiful,
want what is good – and do the opposite of everything!

Joseph Conrad

June 19th

A man always has two reasons
for doing anything: a good reason and
the real reason.

John Pierpont Morgan

June 20th

A wise woman learns in time
to admire her husband even without a reason.

Margot Hielscher

June 21st

The fame of some contemporaries
is also related to the stupidity of their admirers.

Heiner Geißler

June 22nd

After some thought you
find everyone unlikeable.

Laurence Olivier

June 23rd

You only meet the woman of your life once,
but that can be too much.

Gilbert Keith Chesterton

June 24th

First people come into your life,
then they kick your butt.

Therese Giehse

June 25th

Most men would gladly trade
their better half for two younger quarters.

Alan Ayckbourn

June 26th

You never really know a man
until you have divorced him.

Zsa Zsa Gabor

June 27th

There are many people
I would like to miss right now.

Tomi Ungerer

June 28th

Nothing comforts us about the coming
of some people but the hope of their going.

Marie von Ebner-Eschenbach

June 29th

Never do people generate as much happiness as when they say goodbye.

Georg Kreisler

June 30th

When we say goodbye, there is always the fear that we will meet again.

Christian Morgenstern

July

July 1st

When we look at our
daily tasks in the morning,
it is easier to go back to bed.

William Burroughs

July 2nd

My husband is the most effective
sleep aid that I know of.

Judy Garland

July 3rd

Men would be completely superfluous
if vibrators could mow lawns.

Janet Jackson

July 4th

The men of today are also no longer
what they have never been.

Kylie Minogue

July 5th

Men are often as young as they feel,
but never as important.

🗨 *Simone de Beauvoir*

July 6th

Men would gladly let women have
the last word if they could be sure
that it really is the last word.

🗨 *Warren Beatty*

July 7th

The fact that the smarter one gives in
establishes the world domination of women.

🗨 *Erich Mühsam*

July 8th

Whether women are as intelligent as men, I don't know.
But they are certainly not as stupid.

🗨 *Katharina von Medici*

July 9th

Every mistake seems incredibly
stupid when others make it.

Georg Christoph Lichtenberg

July 10th

Everyone make mistakes.
The trick is to make them only
when no one is watching.

Peter Ustinov

July 11th

Those who have made a mistake and
do not correct it will end up being right.

Winston Churchill

July 12th

A man's mistakes are more intelligent
than his attempts to hide them.

Virginia Satir

July 13th

It is always depressing
how intelligent women can be.

Gregor von Rezzori

July 14th

With a woman, you have to be prepared
for everything except the probable.

Hans Söhnker

July 15th

No woman is so bad that
she cannot be a man's better half.

Karl Farkas

July 16th

Marry or marry not,
in any either case you'll regret it.

Socrates

July 17th

When a man steals your wife,
there is no better revenge than
to let him keep her.

💬 *Sacha Guitry*

July 18th

Bachelors know more about women
than married men; if they didn't,
they'd be married too.

💬 *Henry Louis Mencken*

July 19th

Every marriage is an intolerable
encroachment on our freedom.

💬 *Karl Gutzkow*

July 20th

Happiness and blessings
are bad signs.

💬 *Girolamo Savonarola*

July 21st

We never see a person
as they are – and that is their luck.

Joan Baez

July 22nd

You can recognize bad people
by their good excuses.

Marie von Ebner-Eschenbach

July 23rd

Anyone who hates children
and animals can't be all bad.

William Claude "Fields" Dukenfield

July 24th

I love children – especially when they cry,
for then someone takes them away.

Nancy Mitford

July 25th

Your child is not your property.
You will realize that at the latest
when you try to sell it.

Ruth Rendell

July 26th

If you've never been hated by your child,
you've never been a parent.

Bette Davis

July 27th

To be lonely, you have to get married
– to age early, have children.

Liv Ullmann

July 28th

The most reliable way to become unhappy
is to look at yourself in the mirror.

Cathérine Deneuve

July 29th

Everyone has his own way of being unhappy
and one should not disturb them in it.

Aristoteles

July 30th

Laughter and joy are the worst forms
of disturbing the peace.

Cesare Pavese

July 31st

The smile of a child is as
comforting as a snake bite.

Frida Kahlo

”

August

August 1st

If today's suffering is not enough,
add to it yesterday's pain
and tomorrow's fear.

Byron Katie

August 2nd

It's almost always worse than you think.

August Strindberg

August 3rd

If you need cheering up,
think of the infirmities of your friends.

Ginger Rogers

August 4th

Digging a pit for others is exhausting,
but it almost always pays off.

David Herbert Lawrence

August 5th

Some men spend a lifetime in an attempt
to comprehend the complexities of women.
Other preoccupy themselves with somewhat simpler tasks,
such as understanding the theory of relativity!

Albert Einstein

August 6th

You can learn everything from a woman
if you don't ask questions.

William Somerset Maugham

August 7th

The soul of a woman is an open book to me
– written in an incomprehensible language.

Ephraim Kishon

August 8th

Some books only develop their full flavor in the fireplace.

Manuel Vázquez Montalbán

August 9th

Love is a fire that develops
more smoke than heat over the years.

Maurice Chevalier

August 10th

A woman is only a woman,
but a good cigar is a treat.

Elvis Costello

August 11th

Love is the only way
for even the stupid to achieve
a certain greatness.

Honoré de Balzac

August 12th

Words that come from the heart
are usually misspelled.

Allen Ginsberg

August 13th

No one is too poor for it, it costs nothing,
yet accomplishes much and only receives its value
when you pass it on: a bad word.

🗩 *Balthasar Gracián*

August 14th

There are people who are as stingy with their intellect
as others are with their money.

🗩 *Ludwig Börne*

August 15th

It is not from keeping but from giving
that one becomes poor.

🗩 *Cornelius Vanderbilt*

August 16th

Money does not make people happy.
At least not as long as it belongs to others.

🗩 *George Bernard Shaw*

August 17th

Those who want to make others happy
should leave them alone.

Paul Theroux

August 18th

Unrestrained joie de vivre is the best recipe
for getting on the nerves of others.

Judy Garland

August 19th

Those who encourage others are partly
to blame for their good mood.

Peter Sellers

August 20th

We only hire optimists; they think
salary cuts are opportunities.

John Rockefeller

August 21st

It's true hard work never killed anybody,
but I figure, why take the chance?

Ronald Reagan

August 22nd

It is amazing what you can accomplish
if you do not care who gets the credit.

Harry S. Truman

August 23rd

Those who need a vacation do not deserve one.

Abraham Lincoln

August 24th

Never argue with stupid people,
they will drag you down to their level
and then beat you with experience.

Mark Twain

August 25th

Exams are so awful because
the biggest jerk can ask more questions
than the smartest person can answer.

Charles Caleb Colton

August 26th

The empty vessel makes the loudest sound.

Platon

August 27th

The advantage of being stupid is
that you won't be asked for advice.

Edgar Allen Poe

August 28th

After all, good advice helps
the one who gives it.

Balthasar Gracián

August 29th

The dull man who doesn't speak
is more bearable than the stupid one who does.

Jean de la Bruyère

August 30th

There is nothing more annoying than people
who want to talk to you.

Ernest Hemingway

August 31st

Men are capable of talking hours on end
over only one subject; women do it
and don't even require a subject.

Curt Goetz

September

September 1st

Loyalty is only fun in the beginning.

Juliette Gréco

September 2nd

Loyalty is the inability
to transform longing into action.

Louis-Nicolas Vauquelin

September 3rd

Sex at age 90 is like
trying to shoot pool with a rope.

George Burns

September 4th

One of the best remedies for growing old is
snoozing behind the wheel of a moving car.

Juan Manuel Fangio

September 5th

People who drive slowly are ugly
and have contagious diseases.

Ayrton Senna

September 6th

You can't treat a car like a human being.
A car requires love.

Walter Röhrl

September 7th

Women do things for their appearance that any
secon-hand dealer would go to jail for.

Nick Nolte

September 8th

Men read maps better than women because
only men can understand the concept of an inch
equaling a hundred miles.

Roseanne Barr

September 9th

The man has his Achilles heel
not on his foot, but in his crotch.

🗨 *Barbara Walker*

September 10th

Nothing is more mean than to reduce
a woman to her inner values.

🗨 *Barbara Schöneberger*

September 11th

A wise man never contradicts a woman.
He waits until she does it herself.

🗨 *Humphrey Bogart*

September 12th

Women can become very perceptive
when they are wrong.

🗨 *Artur Rubinstein*

September 13th

Marriage is an attempt to become
at least half as happy as one
has been alone.

Oscar Wilde

September 14th

Nothing makes life as complicated
as the attempt to simplify it.

Woody Allen

September 15th

Those who want to simplify their lives
should not meet my mother.

Barbra Streisand

September 16th

We won't have democracy until there is a vote
in each family on who is the mother.

Willy Brandt

September 17th

The stupidity of governments
should never be underestimated.

Helmut Schmidt

September 18th

All life in the state and society
is based on the tacit assumption
that people do not think.

Karl Kraus

September 19th

A good compromise is
when both parties are dissatisfied.

Larry David

September 20th

Those who enjoy small things
can leave the big ones to me.

Charles Bukowski

September 21st

Deals that let you sleep at night
bring in nothing.

Donald Trump

September 22nd

Success hasn't changed me
– I've always been an arrogant asshole.

Don Wayne Johnson

September 23rd

Success is only half as beautiful
if there is no one who envies you.

Norman Mailer

September 24th

Actually, everything that
you don't see is what is beautiful.

Vincent van Gogh

September 25th

I love people. Just the idea
of sharing a room with one of them
is unbearable to me.

Fjodor Dostojewski

September 26th

The best proof of knowledge of
human nature is quiet homicidal desires.

Frank Sinatra

September 27th

Those who are lonely still have to fear
that someone will come to visit.

Hermann Hesse

September 28th

Good friends are people
who live very far away.

Alfred Hitchcock

September 29th

A true friend is someone
who lends you money and then
passes away.

Steve Martin

September 30th

Fame means, above all,
dying at the right time.

Alfred Polgar

”

October

October 1st

Life begins as a promising secret
and ends as an open bankruptcy.

Nick Leeson

October 2nd

The only thing you can create
without money is debt.

Heinz Schenk

October 3rd

Financial problems are best solved
with other people's money.

Jean Paul Getty

October 4th

Most problems arise during their solution.

Leonardo da Vinci

October 5th

Only those who realize their dream
realize that it was a nightmare.

Marilyn Monroe

October 6th

The more planned people are,
the more effectively chance may strike them.

Friedrich Dürrenmatt

October 7th

Calamities are often two kinds:
misfortune to ourselves,
and good fortune to others.

Ambrose Bierce

October 8th

Happiness comes only from human failure.

Jean Giono

October 9th

Trying to make a person happy
almost always ends up being the opposite.

Zarah Leander

October 10th

Whatever you do,
one day you will regret it.

Thomas von Aquin

October 11th

The best way to apologize is
to expose someone else's guilt.

Bill Clinton

October 12th r

The fastest way to gain self-confidence is
to make other people aware of their shortcomings.

Gene Wilder

October 13th

It would be a joy to live if everyone
was only half as ugly as they are.

Joan Crawford

October 14th

If you want to get along with people,
you can't look too closely.

Otto Flake

October 15th

Unfortunately, you usually look
even older than you alreay feel.

Sophia Loren

October 16th

Once you have looked in the mirror,
you can no longer believe in God.

Elizabeth Taylor

October 17th

May God give you the strength
to ignore the things that
you should change.

💬 *Paul Valéry*

October 18th

Every wish you send to the universe
harasses an angel.

💬 *Kalu Rinpoche*

October 19th

I know that you believe you understand
what you think I said, but I'm not sure you realize
that what you heard is not what I meant.

💬 *Alan Greenspan*

October 20th

Silent people become even more boring
when they start talking.

💬 *Jane Austen*

October 21st

I often quote myself.
It adds spice to my conversation.

George Bernard Shaw

October 22nd

Expertise is the last thing you need
for a lively discussion.

Pierre Augustin Caron de Beaumarchais

October 23rd

Saying the right thing
doesn't make you look good.

Rudolf Valentino

October 24th

Don't tell the truth as long as you can think
of something more interesting.

Karl May

October 25th

If we ourselves do not know what to do,
we should give advice to others.

Robert Neumann

October 26th

Some pleasures lies in
withholding it from others.

Edgar Wallace

October 27th

Giving a man his space is like
giving a dog a computer: he probably won't
be able to use it wisely.

Bette-Jane Raphael

October 28th

The more I see of men
the more I like dogs.

Madame de Staël

October 29th

Fear goats from the front,
horses from behind, and
women from all sides.

🗩 *Anton Tschechow*

October 30th

The development from the ape to the human being
probably happened prematurely.

🗩 *Charles Darwin*

October 31st

Often it does seem such a pity that Noah
and his party did not miss the boat.

🗩 *Mark Twain*

November

November 1st

A rainy day in November is
the perfect foretaste of eternal life.

Maurice Chevalier

November 2nd

When you are born,
everything is too late anyway.

Samuel Beckett

November 3rd

When I was young I thought that money
was the most important thing in life;
now that I am old I know that it is.

Oscar Wilde

November 4th

If a person claims that everything
can be achieved with money, you may be sure
that he has never had any.

Aristoteles Onassis

November 5th

Think about what you lack,
then you won't be bored with what you have.

Ovid

November 6th

Life is an eternal interplay
of taking and keeping.

Henry Ford

November 7th

If you think a weakness can be turned
into a strength, I hate to tell you this,
but that's another weakness.

Jack Handey

November 8th

The great strength of fools is
that they are not afraid to say stupid things.

Jean Cocteau

November 9th

If you want to live with a woman,
you must avoid listening to her.

Billy Wilder

November 10th

Those who know how to be silent
just can't speak properly.

Walter Jens

November 11th

Deep inside every human being
there is something that is even less interesting
than his appearance.

George Sand

November 12th

I never forget a face, but in your case
I'll be glad to make an exception.

Groucho Marx

November 13th

Even insults need to be learned.
The kinder, the deeper they hit.

Martin Walser

November 14th

Look for what brings joy to others.
Then you will realize how you can annoy them.

Roald Dahl

November 15th

Gloating is a never-ending source
of strength and serenity.

Frank Billings Kellogg

November 16th

Cheerfullness ist the most
perfidious way to annoy others.

Liza Minnelli

November 17th

Nothing is as annoying as when people
around you are in a good mood.

Melvin Lasky

November 18th

If you want to feel bad,
all you have to do is invite your friends.

Sidonie-Gabrielle Colette

November 19th

You have more friends than you fear.

Agatha Christie

November 20th

Punctuality is the art of estimating correctly
how late the others will be.

Bob Hope

November 21st

Wit is something
you don't think of until 24 hours later.

Mark Twain

November 22nd

What lasts a long time doesn't get better.

Ricarda Huch

November 23rd

Men achieve their greatest efficiency
in doing things that do not need
to be done at all.

Brooke Shields

November 24th

Whoever builds a house for his wife
should not forget the trapdoor.

Antonio Gaudí

November 25th

God created woman to tame man.

Voltaire

November 26th

The ideal husband understands
every word his wife doesn't say.

Alfred Hitchcock

November 27th

In the past, sacrifices
were offered at the altar.
This has not changed.

Michael Heltau

November 28th

Love: A temporary insanity curable
by marriage.

Ambrose Bierce

November 29th

Once you're over the hill,
it quickly goes downhill
from there, all by itself.

Johanna Spyri

November 30th

Would you mind taking
your thoughts to the grave?

Minette Walters

”

December

December 1st

The optimist says that tomorrow is another day.
The pessimist knows that this is true.

Paul Claudel

December 2nd

Even the greatest effort is in vain in the end.

Nazim Hikmet

December 3rd

The good thing about winter is that
no men walk around with short pants.

Martina Navratilova

December 4th

Moons and years pass,
but bad taste remains.

Coco Chanel

December 5th

Women who want to be the first to wear every fashion creation
are usually the ones who should leave it alone.

Yves Saint-Laurent

December 6th

A man running after a hat
is not half as ridiculous as a man
running after a woman.

Gilbert Keith Chesterton

December 7th

First, God created man, then he created woman.
Then God felt sorry for men
and gave them tobacco.

Mark Twain

December 8th

Only a stupid person can be healthy.

Thomas Mann

December 9th

A cheerful look can encourage
the biggest fool.

Romy Schneider

December 10th

Praise makes bad people worse
and good people unbearable.

Hermann Hesse

December 11th

Laugh at life and it growls back.

Jean Paul

December 12th

No matter what you did or didn't do,
you will regret it.

Giovanni Boccaccio

December 13th

I refuse to join any club

that would have me as a member.

Groucho Marx

December 14th

Some people think they are popular,

but people have only become accustomed to their ways.

Upton Sinclair

December 15th

Be yourself

– and as far away as possible.

Ruth Rendell

December 16th

The world is full of wonders

that get on your nerves.

Arundhati Roy

December 17th

No matter how many qualties we have,
the world pays attention mainly to our bad ones.

Jean-Baptiste Poquelin

December 18th

No character is so bad
that it cannot still be corrupted.

Hermann Kesten

December 19th

Even the greatest effort
is in vain in the end.

Édith Piaf

December 20th

It's only since I've loved
that I've known that that's no use either.

Iris Murdoch

December 21st

The call to charity is particularly
inconvenient to me around Christmas.

August Strindberg

December 22nd

Whatever you give
will be resented.

Otto von Bismarck

December 23rd

Gifts are the only form of revenge
left for cultured people.

Peter Ustinov

December 24th

A family reunion is not only the fault of those
who host it, but also of those
who do not prevent it.

Karl Kraus

December 25th

At Christmas is when you least understand
what men are good for.

Donna Leon

December 26th

You do not age during the year,
but during the Christmas days.

Greta Garbo

December 27th

Those who still laugh heartily in old age
make themselves unpopular with their heirs.

Aristoteles Onassis

December 28th

The annoying thing about getting old
is that you have to pretented to have fun.

Marcello Mastroianni

December 29th

You don't change,
you don't get better,
you just get older.

Paul Newman

December 30th

The new year often starts before
you've gotten through the old one.

Elizabeth Taylor

December 31st

Afterwards, you are usually
even dumber than before.

Astrid Lindgren

Here are 100 more mean quotes waiting for you:

www.timreichel.com/quotes-dry-humor-gift

Keywords

Topics

Are you looking for a suitable quote on a specific topic? In this overview you will find the right words for every occasion.

Love and Sex 8.1., 9.1., 10.1., 12.1., 28.1., 23.4., 29.4., 12.5., 25.6., 3.7., 9.8., 11.8., 12.8., 1.9., 2.9., 3.9., 6.9., 9.9., 25.9., 28.11., 14.12., 19.12., 20.12., 21.12.

Friendship 15.1., 16.1., 4.5., 24.5., 24.6., 3.8., 28.9., 29.9., 14.11., 18.11., 22.12., 23.12.

Guests 15.1., 31.1., 11.2., 12.2., 13.2., 4.5., 13.6., 14.6., 28.6., 29.6. 30.6., 27.9., 18.11., 19.11., 20.11.

Fashion and Beauty 29.1., 15.5., 27.5., 11.6., 12.6., 28.7., 7.9., 10.9., 24.9., 13.10., 14.10., 16.10., 23.10., 12.11., 3.12., 4.12., 5.12.

Profession and Career 2.1., 3.1., 4.1., 6.1., 2.2., 4.3., 5.3., 6.3., 7.3., 21.3., 11.4., 12.4., 13.4., 18.5., 23.5., 3.6., 4.6., 5.7., 10.7., 11.7., 4.8., 20.8., 21.8., 22.8., 23.8., 6.10., 6.11., 10.12.

Money 5.1., 25.7., 26.7., 13.8., 14.8., 15.8., 16.8., 20.8., 21.9., 29.9., 1.10., 2.10., 3.10., 3.11., 4.11., 6.11., 27.12.

Politics 6.1., 21.1., 25.2., 15.3., 22.3., 2.4., 3.4., 8.4., 10.4., 18.4., 3.6., 5.6., 9.6., 21.6., 7.7., 11.7., 21.8., 22.8., 16.9., 17.9., 18.9., 19.9., 11.10., 22.10., 14.12.

Stupidity 6.1., 7.1., 8.1., 15.1., 22.1., 21.2., 27.2., 31.3., 6.4., 7.4., 8.4., 14.4., 15.4., 8.5., 25.5., 2.6., 3.6., 8.6., 17.6., 8.7., 9.7., 11.8., 14.8., 24.8., 25.8., 26.8., 27.8., 29.8., 17.9., 8.11., 8.12., 9.12., 31.12.

Religion and God 16.1., 17.1., 3.2., 2.3., 1.5., 2.5., 3.5., 4.5., 5.5., 6.5., 15.5., 16.5., 20.7., 16.10., 17.10., 18.10., 19.10., 31.10., 1.11., 25.11., 27.11., 7.12., 16.12., 21.12., 25.12., 26.12.

Age 10.2., 11.2., 22.2., 23.2., 24.2., 25.2., 9.3., 10.3, 4.4., 27.7., 3.9., 4.9., 1.10., 15.10., 26.12., 27.12., 28.12., 29.12.

Farewell 12.1., 13.1., 13.2., 4.4., 5.4., 26.6., 27.6., 28.6., 29.6., 30.6.

Postscript

About the Book

This book is not a classic collection of quotes with a claim to completeness, but a personal compilation that has only one aim: to provide you with a pool of original – albeit wicked – quotes. I have therefore selected the individual quotes in such a way that together they will have the most entertaining effect for you. I have taken care to cover as wide a range of authors as possible to ensure a dynamic mix of content.

Each quote has been carefully researched and checked several times for authenticity. To do this, I consulted classic reference works, original texts and online sources and had the results checked several times by third parties. Nevertheless, errors may have occurred during this laborious process. If you notice anything unusual while reading or if you have specific comments on a particular quotation, please send me a message on kontakt@studienscheiss.de. I read every e-mail and take all comments seriously.

By the way: This book was produced fairly and to a high standard by our Impact publishing house. We work with regional designers and lecturers and have our hardcover books produced entirely in Germany. We treat all partners involved in the production chain fairly – and pay them fairly. All of them are small and medium-sized companies who put their heart and soul into their work and with whom we share a common goal: to create high-quality products that make our readers happy.

Our books are created under sustainable production conditions, protect the environment and promote the regional economy. And that's exactly what you're supporting when you buy this book.

Thank you very much for that.

About the Author

Dr. Tim Reichel, born in 1988, is an author, scientist and entrepreneur. After graduating from high school, he studied industrial engineering at RWTH Aachen University and then stayed on to do his doctorate. There he supervises industry-related research projects and deals with the topics of sustainability and resource efficiency. He completed his doctorate at the Faculty of Georesources and Materials Engineering in September 2018.

He has been working as a student advisor and coordinator of an examination board for ten years. He coaches students, advises them on difficulties in their studies, writes examination regulations and supports accreditation procedures. In June 2014, Tim founded his first company: Studienscheiss. With this platform, he helps millions of students and people interested in education across Germany to study happily and successfully in order to do really well in their future careers.

In his blog, Tim regularly publishes articles on the topics of time management, motivation and personal development. He is also a columnist for Der Spiegel and writes numerous specialist articles on his focus topics as a freelance author. His book "Busy is the new stupid" was named a business bestseller by Manager Magazin in June 2020. In addition to his activities as a publisher and writer, Tim works as a speaker and offers training seminars and mentoring programs.

This is Tim

Thank You!

I would like to thank all the readers of my Studienscheiss blog. Without you and your huge support, my blog and this book would not exist. You are the best community there is in the German-speaking world and I love writing for you. Thank you for motivating me, criticizing me and always standing behind me. Thank you for being there.

I could never have written this book on my own. That's why I'd especially like to thank the people who helped me along the way: Hannah, Delia, Sina, Melanie, Sara, Charlotte and Sajoscha.

Thank you for putting up with me and supporting me in every difficult situation. Even when I was being annoying and bitchy or just being stupid.

Your reliability, your patience and your commitment are incredible and anything but taken for granted. I really appreciate that – and thank you all from the bottom of my heart.

Tim Reichel, December 2023

Gift

Here are 100 more mean quotes waiting for you:

www.timreichel.com/quotes-dry-humor-gift

Thank You!

Printed in Great Britain
by Amazon

55146448R00079